ART FOR AUTISM

Enhancing the Lives of Children

A Field Guide
By Elissa Anne Parkerson, MAPC

This book is dedicated to:

My family: Ivan & Jessica Neel, Rachel & Jessica Parkerson;
All the wonderful children that have worked so diligently and cooperatively
During the experientials in this book…and
The parents who have allowed me the privilege of working with
Their children.

My Mentor, Barbara Bagan, Ph.D., ATR-BC
&
Dixie Ciccarelli, MAPC, LAC, ATR
Paula Artac, D Min, ATR-BC, CEAT

All of whom inspired, and shared their wealth of knowledge into the world of
Expressive Arts Therapy

TABLE OF CONTENTS

I.   **INTRODUCTION** **5-7**

II.   **GLOSSARY OF TERMS** **8-12**

III.   **CLAY EXPERIENTIALS** **13-19**

        Clay Animals 14-15

        Clay Pots 16

        Pueblo Village 17-19

IV.   **MULTIMODAL EXPERIENTIALS** **20-37**

        Creating Myself 22-23

        Paper Mosaics 24-25

        My Name Is A 26-28

        Pine Cone Grass Pets 29-30

        Scribble Doodle Sand Art 31-32

        Twig People 33-34

        Paper Mache Bowls 35-37

V.   **GROUP EXPERIENTIALS** **38-44**

        Adobe Bricks 35-36

        Tree Branch Painting on Floor Cloth 39-40

        Mandalas 43-44

VI.   **PAINTING EXPERIENTIALS** **45-52**

        Painting With Dots 46

        Easel Painting 47-48

        Half & Half Paintings 49-50

        Creative T-Shirts 51-52

TABLE OF CONTENTS CONTINUED

VII.   **SPECIAL OCCASSIONS EXPERIENTIALS**...**53-57**

   Painting & Collage Christmas Cards 54-55

   Woven Paper Father's Day Cards...56-57

VIII.   **REFERENCES & Websites**..**58-60**

Scribble Doodle Apple Tree

A collaboration; instructor and 4 year old boy with Autism;
The importance of parallel work to enhance and encourage many skill areas.

Introduction

Celebrate every accomplishment, no matter how small; focus on what the child can do...

It is my belief as a professional counselor, educator, and expressive arts facilitator, that the social, moral, intellectual and emotional potential of each child with autism be cultivated and guided with dignity and integrity. Each day a child is given opportunities to engage in self expression leads the child on a life long path to success and well being. Expressive Arts can be used as a complimentary therapy along with Applied Behavior Analysis (ABA), as a systematic approach to helping individuals acquire socially useful behaviors or change problematic ones (Lovaas & Smith, 1989); and will create positive outcomes for most individuals with autism and significantly enhance their development. Expressive Arts is not used as a replacement therapy, but can be designed to enhance and encourage creativity. Often children with Autism are non-verbal, and art can be used as an effective method in reaching the child, and fostering positive social interactions.

The manifestations of autism vary considerably across individuals and within an individual child over time; when the child is allowed to explore and express him/herself using a positive approach; and given opportunities that encourage development; the child will flourish. Studies have shown that using art can be an effective method of breaking through the barriers of autism (Banks, Davis, Howard & McLaughlin, 1993); and is now being recognized as an important feature in treatment when combined with one or more of the Early Intervention Methods (Volkmar & Pauls, 2004).

My focus of studies in Early Childhood, Special Education, Psychology, Applied Behavior Analysis, and Expressive Arts have blended together to give me the knowledge and tools in order to assist children with Autism in becoming successful.

Allowing experiences for the creative art process to occur in teaching and/or therapy sessions using the natural environment as the third teacher (inspired by the Reggio Emilia Approach to learning; Edwards, Gandini, & Foreman, 1998); has and continues to give me insight into the world of Autism.

Empirical evidence supports the benefits of combining treatments as symptoms vary with each individual; art can provide a nonverbal, symbolic way for the child to express feelings and emotions which may help to alleviate many of the negative symptoms of the disorder (Banks, 1993), and increase an array of skills that are often *hidden* beneath the surface of children with Autism. Art helps to develop language/communication, social, fine motor, perceptual motor, eye contact, tactile/kinesthetic awareness, attention span, spatial relationships, concept development, cause and effect, sequencing, self expression, self esteem and self efficacy (Flowers, 1992). Art can also be a useful tool to enhance the assessment process, by creating an environment that is more comfortable and motivational for the child, which can allow the child opportunities to display skills that may go unrecognized.

Expressive Arts is not your typical "cookie cutter" art, it is art that is created by the child, not the adult, teacher, parent or provider; it is a process the child goes through; the adult or peer can provide guidance and interaction which is a part of healthy language and social development for a child with autism. Vygotsky's theory, the idea that potential for cognitive development depends upon the "zone of proximal development" (ZPD): a level of development attained when children engage in social behavior. Full development of the ZPD depends upon full social interaction; and the range of skill that can be developed with adult guidance or peer collaboration exceeds what can be attained alone. Most of the original ZPD work was done in the context of language learning in children (Vygotsky, 1978); which provides a framework similar to that of ABA (in my opinion), the results are the same, the child learns the language and communication skills, but in a more natural way. Vygotsky's theory is recognized and useful in my style of teaching, facilitating, and/or providing counseling for children with Autism; allowing the child to do as much as possible on his/her own, close observation, and use of scaffolding to complete the process (Jones & Reynolds, 1992).

Art opportunities can happen anywhere, anytime; in nature, watching bees pollinate the flowers, at home baking, playing music, dancing, at school during playtime with sand and/or water, tree branches can be used as paintbrushes, pine cones, grass seeds, dirt and water can be used to make a 'Pine Cone Pet' (one of my science/art projects), clay, adobe bricks out of dirt, sand, straw, water and the abundant sunshine to make a small structure or miniature house. Art is math, science, history... art is everywhere; there are no mistakes in art. Using art techniques can be a helpful tool in overcoming sensory issues dealing with textures of certain foods; art provides a positive approach to increase, and encourage healthy eating habits. Art can help develop awareness of critical skills necessary for transition to the workplace ad career goals.

This book is to share and bring awareness of the importance of implementing Expressive Arts into teaching, curriculum design, counseling/therapy sessions, social groups/peer play, and everyday life; discover at least one interest in particular of the individual, and build on that interest with the help of art, as this will provide a stepping stone that leads toward a path of success.

"If the only tool you use is a hammer, then every problem will start to look like a nail".
Abraham Maslow

GLOSSARY OF TERMS

Abstract concepts: Intangible; includes feelings (e.g., love, nervousness). Children with Autism receive a constant flow of visual and auditory information which facilitate the development of concepts. Abstract concepts are not developed easily; therefore, alternative strategies have to be used in order for development of concepts to occur.

Concept Development: A concept is a mental representation, image or idea of tangible and concrete objects (e.g., a chair, a dog) and intangible ideas and feelings (e.g., colors and emotions). A skill is that ability to do something (e.g. tying a shoe, using vision to find an object.

Concrete concepts: Relate to objects or things that are tangible (e.g., a car, a chair).

Semi-concrete concepts: Relate to an action, color, position, or something that can be demonstrated but not held in one's hand (e.g., jumping, behind, red).

Spatial Abilities: Those perceptual/cognitive abilities that enable one to deal effectively with spatial relations, visual-spatial tasks, orientation of objects in space, etc.

Spatial Cognition: Refers to the general ability to find one's way in a complex environment.

Spatial Orientation: The ability to orient oneself in space relative to objects and events. Awareness of self location (Reber & Reber, 2001).

Fine Motor Skills: Muscular coordination in cases where delicate control is needed (2001).

Integrated Arts approach or Intermodal (also known as Multimodal) Therapy: Involves two or more expressive therapies to foster awareness, encourage emotional growth, and enhance relationships with others. Intermodal therapy distinguishes itself from its closely allied disciplines of art therapy, music therapy, dance/movement therapy and drama therapy by being grounded in the interrelatedness of the arts. It is based on a variety of orientations, including arts as therapy, art psychotherapy, and the use of arts for traditional healing. All of the expressive therapies involve actions, and have inherent differences; visual expression is conducive to more private, isolated work, and may lend itself to enhancing the process of individuation. Music often taps feeling and may lend itself to socialization when people collaborate in song or in simultaneously playing instruments. Dance/movement offer opportunities to interact and form relationships. In other words, each form of expressive therapy has its unique properties and roles in therapeutic work depending on its application, practitioner, client, setting, and objectives (Knill *etal*, 1995).

Kinesthetic Awareness: Encompasses the body's abilities to coordinate motion (such as pitching a baseball) and the body's awareness of where it is in time and space (think dancing). When you see a troupe of ballet dancers moving together it is largely kinesthetic awareness that allows them to move in harmony together instead of bumping into each other. Using a variety of medium to create art and manipulating the materials helps to enhance this skill (http://dictionary.reference.com).

Mandala *(Photograph on Front Cover)***:** The Mandala originates from Tibetan Sanskrit meaning "containing" or "circle-completion" (http://www.mandalas.com). Mandalas can be used to describe any geometric design or pattern that symbolizes metaphysical or symbolic characteristics of the universe. Mandala designs can simply be used as a base for creativity when working with children with autism.

Sensory Integration: Is an innate neurobiological process that refers to the integration and interpretation of environmental stimuli. Children with Autism lack the ability to integrate or organize stimuli appropriately in the brain and may produce varying degrees of problems in development, information processing and behavior. Sensory integration focuses primarily on three basic senses: *Tactile* system is the largest sensory system in the body and plays a vital role in human behavior, both physical and mental.

Touch sensations flow throughout the entire nervous system and influence every neural process to some extent. Without a great deal of tactile stimulation of the body, the nervous system tends to become "unbalanced." This helps to explain why the tactile system is involved in most disorders of the human brain; *Vestibular* system is the sensory system that responds to the position of the head in relation to gravity and accelerated or decelerated movement. There are two types of vestibular receptors in the inner ear in a structure called the labyrinth. One type of receptor responds to the force of gravity. The other types of receptors are in the semicircular canals in the ear. These canals are responsible for our sense of movement; and *Proprioceptive* system consists of sensory information caused by contraction and stretching of muscles and by bending, straightening, pulling and compression of the joints between the bones. Because there are so many muscles and joints in the body, the proprioceptive system is almost as large as the tactile system. Most proprioceptive input is processed in areas of the brain that do not produce conscious awareness. Without good automatic responses, such things as eye-hand coordination is very difficult (OCLDA: Sensory and Perceptual Systems).

Tactile defensiveness: A condition in which an individual is extremely sensitive to light touch. When the tactile system is immature and working improperly, abnormal neural signals are sent to the cortex in the brain which can interfere with other brain processes; this in turn causes the brain to be overly stimulated and may lead to excessive brain activity, which can neither be turned off nor organized. Some children may be hypersensitive to vestibular stimulation and have fearful reactions to ordinary movement activities (e.g., swings, slides, ramps, incline). They may also have trouble learning to climb or descend stairs or hills; and they may be apprehensive walking or crawling on uneven or unstable surfaces. This type of over stimulation in the brain can make it difficult for an individual to organize ones behavior and concentrate, and may lead to a negative emotional response to touch sensations.

Incorporating art as a method of treatment for the child with Autism could alleviate many areas of sensory deprivation by providing tools, and opportunities to express their needs, and to anticipate the behavior of others when it is regulated by external, observable factors rather than by mental states (1995).

Some of the experientials can be created with music and movement, use your imagination and allow any child to participate in any way possible...

NO CHILD SHOULD BE LEFT BEHIND!

Twig People - Experiential – The Dancer

CLAY EXPERIENTIALS

Animals
Clay Pots
Pueblo Village

This is a 7 year old boy with autism using the clay tools. Using the tools can
minimize resistance to touching the clay, and ease the child into
eventually manipulating the clay with enjoyment.

EXPERIENTIAL: Clay Animals

OBJECTIVES:

- Increase language and communication skills
- Increase fine motor skills
- Enhance sensory motor skills
- Improve tactile & concept awareness
- Build self-efficacy
- Enhance self-esteem
- Positive self-awareness & self-image
- Expression of self
- Leads the child in a positive direction

AGE GROUP(S):   5 & up

MATERIALS: Terre Cotta, white or grey clay. I use AMACO Brand and/or Crayola white clay (American Art Clay Co., Inc.); these are my favorite brands of clay and made in USA, non-toxic - very easy to clean up.

Pictures or photos of animals, magazines and books; Wooden clay tools; bowl or squeeze bottle of water; paper towels.

ENVIRONMENT: Inside or outside table; outside work area is more desirable when weather permits. Work area should be free of clutter.

DIRECTIONS: Have children get a chunk of clay or have pre-portioned bags to hand out. Talk about the different animals that children are familiar and unfamiliar with; use the photos or magazine pictures to give the children some ideas. This also allows the children to experience learning about different species of animals. Work side by side with the children and be available to assist if needed.

Have children manipulate the clay into a ball to begin shaping. After the animals are formed, direct children to carve features with the tools. Allow to dry overnight. Give the option of painting the animal when dry; I like Folk Art iridescent paint (under $2.50/bottle).

NOTES: Clay tools are very useful for the hesitant or resistant child with sensory issues. The child is able to ease into working the clay using hands and tools, instead of having to work only by touching with their hands. Eventually the child will work the clay by hand.

Clay is an extremely useful tool when working with children with sensory issues. When a child with Autism manipulates the clay, he/she is being provided with an opportunity that can have a positive effect in many areas of development.

EXPERIENTIAL: Clay Pots

OBJECTIVES:

- Increase language and communication skills
- Increase fine motor skills
- Enhance tactile/kinesthetic awareness
- Develop conceptual awareness

AGE GROUP(S):   5 and older

MATERIALS: AAMCO Terre Cotta Clay; magazine pictures or photos of various clay pots. Wooden or plastic clay tools, bowl of water and paper towels.

ENVIRONMENT: Old wood table or plastic work table

DIRECTIONS: Allow child to get a hunk of clay or have pre-proportioned bags of clay if working in a group. Direct the child to form a ball and then smooth the surface with hands and some water. Show how you push your thumb down into the center of the ball of clay to form a bowl or elongated shape. Then start to shape your pot by pinching with fingers; there are many different styles of pots to make. Show the child how to carve designs on the pot using the tools.

NOTES: Terre Cotta, white or gray clay can be used depending on whether or not you desire to paint the pots or leave natural. Discuss with child or group about many cultures that hand make pots and their uses. Have some library books or art books of pottery available for children to look through. You can tell a short story about pottery before you begin the experiential.

EXPERIENTIAL: Adobe or Pueblo Indian Village ~ this is a project that can take several days, and can be left out and other items can be added.

OBJECTIVES:

- Increase language and communication skills
- Increase fine motor skills
- Enhance tactile /kinesthetic awareness
- Develop conceptual awareness
- Increase knowledge of another culture
- Sequencing
- Gain Concepts of Spatial Relationships
- Building on social relationships

AGE GROUP(S): 5 and older – can be use with one child at a time or in a group.
This is a continuous project, and not one that can be completed in a day.

MATERIALS: Square or rectangular piece of any type of wood to use for your village (size will vary depending on whether you are doing this as a group project or individual). Coarse sand is preferable, but you can use whatever type you like to spread over the glue to resemble dirt.

Terre cotta clay, small twigs, miscellaneous animals and figurines, bowl of water, clay tools, pieces of scrap wood, glue, straw or hay, and flat wooden toothpicks.

There are many books available at local libraries with colorful and realistic photos of the villages, people, tools they use, animals, ovens, ladders, and sand. (Use a rough grain of sand with a reddish color for a more realistic ground; can be bought at Home Depot for a few dollars).

ENVIRONMENT: Outside or inside work table; the table should be long enough to support the slab of wood, or piece of heavy cardboard; work area and supplies.

DIRECTIONS: Discuss the project, read through the books with the child so he/she is able to visualize the village and how the Indians lived. You can either start by spreading glue on the slab of wood, or then put sand over the glue. Then start forming the buildings, different sizes can be made and stacked as shown in the books. Show the child how to form a square with the clay. Make as many buildings as desired, use the twigs to place through the tops of the buildings – similar to how the beams were used by the Indians. The toothpicks are used to make ladders. Michael's sells a bag of small wooden strips that can be used in place of the toothpicks.

NOTES: I did this experiential with several children with autism ranging from ages 5 and older; we continued working on the project and adding new items to it over the course of several months. This was a wonderful experiential for all of us. The children seemed to enjoy playing in the village each time they came in for an Expressive Arts session; small animals and other items were continuously added to the scene. This is an important project to help build on family relations and values; and helping to develop family concepts whereas children with Autism have difficulty relating to the importance of contributing to the family unit.

RESOURCES: The Pueblo Indians (Natives Peoples)
The Pueblo by Charlotte Yue

Pueblo Village: collaboration with several children and Arts Facilitator

MULTIMODAL EXPERIENTIALS

Creating Myself (Inspired by Flat Stanley)
Paper Mosaics
My Name is a….cutting/pasting/decorating
Pine Cone Grass Pets
Scribble Doodle Sand Art
Twig Dolls
Paper Mache Bowls

This Scribble Doodle was described as "birds" by the young boy.

Created by a 5 year old boy with Autism and his older sister.

EXPERIENTIAL: Creating Myself (Inspired by Flat Stanley)

AGE GROUP(S):   4 & Up

OBJECTIVES:

- Build self-efficacy
- Enhance self efficacy/esteem
- Positive self-awareness & self-image
- Expression of self
- Leads the child in a positive direction
- Increase fine motor skills

MATERIALS: Paper Doll cut out on oak tag or card stock (blank), white, tan, or brown; a variety of yarns, ribbons, buttons, paper clothes, shoes, and any other items you can use to decorate yourself. You can download the Flat Stanley template and cut out, but use the back side that does not have any features on it. Having the blank one allows and encourages creativity. You can show the child sample pictures if you want.

ENVIRONMENT: Table top or counter area. Have work area free of clutter so you can have plenty of room to display items on paper or plastic shallow plates or containers for easy access. You can have plates labeled for each group of items. I like to incorporate words and sentences whenever possible to assist children with autism to have language learning opportunities.

DIRECTIONS: Talk with the child about how he/she would like to decorate the paper doll, show the child all the things available to use. Encourage the child to incorporate details; make a face on the doll, add hair and clothing.

NOTES: This is a great activity to do with an individual or a group, it is a lot of fun to work parallel to the child to encourage the child and have conversation about what you are doing.

SOURCE: Inspired by Flat Stanley by Jeff Brown

EXPERIENTIAL: Paper Mosaics

OBJECTIVES:

- Increase fine motor skills
- Enhance and encourage creativity
- Develop conceptual awareness
- Increase language and communication skills
- Develop form discrimination
- Increase perceptual motor skills
- Increase attention span

AGE GROUP(S): 3 & older

MATERIALS: 5 X 7 sheet of white card stock or 8 ½ X 11, torn or cut up pieces of paper,
I use handmade paper, magazine pictures, anything with different textures and colors. The paper can be torn or cut into different shapes and sizes. Michael's has handmade paper for about $4 a pack, or other types of cardstock paper. The handmade paper is excellent to use for this and makes beautiful mosaics. Glue sticks or liquid glue on a plate with cue tips, or let the child use the bottle.

ENVIRONMENT: Inside table top free of clutter, have papers in several different bowls or containers for the child to feel and choose whatever ones he/she likes.

DIRECTIONS: Talk about what you will be making, work alongside the child. Simply glue individual pieces of paper onto the large sheet of card stock. Arrange in any manner desired. You can create a pattern or abstract.

This is a project to let loose and do whatever you want. The child can use as many pieces of torn or cut paper as desired; there are very few rules to this one. Basically don't pour out the whole bottle of glue.

NOTES: This is a great project for the child to create his/her own shapes and designs. You can also have pre-cut shapes available as well as paper and scissors if the child wants to cut their own shapes. Be flexible. This is a very calming activity. During an activity with a 9 year old boy with Autism, he kept trying to find the matching pieces, I encouraged him to work with a variety by explaining it is not a puzzle, it is a mosaic; not to take away from his creativity, and we were working on expanding interests.

EXPERIENTIAL: My Name Is A….

OBJECTIVES:

- Increase fine motor skills
- Encourage creativity
- Develop conceptual awareness
- Increase language and communication skills
- Develop form discrimination
- Increase perceptual motor skills
- Increase attentions span
- Increase self esteem/self efficacy

AGE GROUP(S):   5 & older

MATERIALS: Sheet of white paper, cardstock or heavy copy paper; markers, glitter, colored pencils, and scissors. You can use anything to decorate.

ENVIRONMENT: Inside work table with plenty of room to lay out supplies.

DIRECTIONS: Instruct child to fold the paper in half the long way, and then write his/her name over the folded area; write the name in cursive as large as you can. Then cut around the letters starting from the open end. You can cut into the fold in some areas for more intricate design but be careful not to cut all of it. Then have the child open up the paper. Ask the child what he/she thinks it looks like. Decorate and have fun!

This is an awesome group experiential and I've used it with many children. One 9-year old boy with autism said he hated art prior to this project and stated that he did not want to participate. However, once the activity got started he joined the others and ended up spending over an hour on his name which turned out to be a praying mantis.

NOTES: If you are working with children who do not write in cursive, then just do hand over hand with them as it needs to be done in cursive. Remember, there is nothing wrong with helping a child, just allow the child to do as much as he/she can and observe for your time to step in and assist to prevent frustration. This is an awesome group experiential and I've used it with many children. One 9-year old boy with autism said he hated art prior to this project and stated that he did not want to participate. However, once the activity got started he joined the others and ended up spending over an hour on his name which turned out to be a praying mantis.

SOURCE: This experiential is taken from Principles, Techniques and Practices of Expressive Arts Therapy at Ottawa University taught by Dixie Ciccarelli.

My name is a butterfly, as described by a 5 year old boy.

EXPERIENTIAL: Pine Cone Grass Pets

OBJECTIVES:

- ✚ To develop an understanding of how things grow
- ✚ Develop concept of awareness
- ✚ Increase language and communication
- ✚ Increase fine motor skills
- ✚ Increase tactile/kinesthetic awareness

AGE GROUP(S):   Any age is appropriate. The younger the child, the more assistance the child will need. This is a great opportunity to do parallel, cooperative work, incorporate science into learning while watching something grow.

MATERIALS: Pine cones, dirt, grass seeds, water, a tray or bowl depending on how many you will make; spray bottle for water. Netting that fruits and vegetable come in or you can buy some. It is called bird netting and you can purchase at Home Depot for a few dollars. Use netting if you would like to hang your pine cones up outside. Otherwise, just use a container.

It is a good idea to have a book or two about things that grow and talk to the child about what you will be doing.

ENVIRONMENT: Outside, you can work on the ground or at a table; this can also be done inside.

DIRECTIONS: Decide on how many you will make, simply place the pine cone in a container or netting, sprinkle a little dirt in the grooves of the pine cone and mist with water. Then sprinkle some grass seeds, add some more dirt and spray with water again. Talk with the child about how long it will take for the grass to start growing. I use a calendar as a reference point and you can mark off each day.

NOTES: Remember to water daily, it takes about 5-7 days, after which you will have about several inches of growth. This is an amazing project for children and adults as well. The pine cone(s) can be hung up on a patio area, or placed in a clay pot. There are many options. If the clay pots are used, the child can decorate the pot, and used for a Mother's day gift.

EXPERIENTIAL: Scribble Doodle Sand Art

OBJECTIVES:

- Increase fine motor skills
- Enhance tactile/kinesthetic awareness
- Increase concept development
- Increase spatial ability
- Develop language/communication skills
- Social development

AGE GROUP(S):   3 and older – This is a great group activity!

MATERIALS: #2 pencils, glue, colored sand, small funnel and spoon, white paper, or other colors, you can use black paper but the child will need to scribble with a white or yellow pencil.

ENVIRONMENT: Table top, outside or inside; table may be covered

DIRECTIONS: Direct the child to start scribbling, work alongside to model. Just have fun with it! For older children, you can ask them to hold their paper up and turn in different directions to look for patterns, designs, or shapes.
After the child is done with the scribble doodle, direct the child to drizzle glue on the design. Then sprinkle the sand onto the glue

NOTES: Sand can be in bags or small trays; encourage child to use the spoon and funnel to enhance fine motor skills, have materials available for easy access for children to move freely around a table if the child prefers to stand. You can buy a box of sand at Michaels for about $5.95 which contains 6 different colors.

Play Classical or Spanish Guitar music during this experiential.

Scribble Doodle to be free!

EXPERIENTIAL: Twig People (Inspired by Karen Laura Miller's – Love You Doll).

OBJECTIVES:

- Increase fine motor skills
- Enhance tactile/kinesthetic awareness
- Increase concept development
- Increase spatial ability
- Develop language/communication skills
- Pride in ownership

AGE GROUP(S):   5 & older – Younger children can do this, but may need additional help from an adult.

MATERIALS: A variety of twigs; yarn, glue, buttons, googly eyes, felt, ribbons. You can also use a hot glue gun and or tacky glue works well with the items.

ENVIRONMENT: Outside or inside, table large enough to lay out all items.

DIRECTIONS: You can have the child look for his own stick, or you can have some already available. You want to find ones that basically look like a stick figure; one long straight piece with 2 other pieces that can be legs, the arms can be added. Or you can just use whatever stick you like.
Most likely you will have to help the child get started wrapping the yarn, once they start, they will really get into it. Then you just add whatever you want to your doll. This is your own creation, so have fun with it!

A 9 year old boy with Autism and his Twig Person

This was a group project !

EXPERIENTIAL: Paper Mache Bowls

OBJECTIVES:

- Increase fine motor skills
- Enhance tactile/kinesthetic awareness
- Increase concept development
- Increase spatial ability
- Develop language/communication skills
- Pride in ownership

AGE GROUP(S):   5 & older – Great activity for a group.

MATERIALS: Paper Mache (can be purchased at Michaels, comes in a packaged roll)
Have pre-cut strips ready to use; bowl of warm water, some paper towels, brown paper bag to work on, and a package of large balloons.
Paints glitter, or anything you would like to use to decorate your bowl. I use iridescent paint that you can get at Michaels or Joanne's. It comes in small bottles and is about $2 a bottle.
The colors are beautiful and vibrant.

ENVIRONMENT: Outside or inside

DIRECTIONS: Discuss with the child what you will be doing; this does require that you help the child. This is a project that you do together. Talk with the child you will be working with about every step. First you will dip a strip into to water and then hold up to let excess water out, then start laying each strip around half of the balloon until it is completely covered.

Repeat each step and create at least 3 layers. The more layers, the stronger the bowl will be. One package is enough for 3 bowls. Allow to dry, and then decorate. This usually takes 2 days to complete.

Paper Mache Bowl by a 5 year old boy with autism.

I drew the dolphins (he requested dolphins) and helped him paint, but he was able to complete 80% of the whole project, and appeared to enjoy doing it!

GROUP EXPERIENTIALS

Adobe Bricks
Tree Branch Painting on Floor Cloth
Mandalas

Tree Branch Painting

Created by 6 year old boy with autism and two younger siblings.

EXPERIENTIAL: Adobe Bricks

OBJECTIVES:

- Increase language and communication skills
- Increase fine motor skills
- Enhance tactile /kinesthetic awareness
- Develop conceptual awareness
- Increase knowledge of another culture
- Develop building techniques
- Sequencing
- Gain concepts of spatial relationships
- Social skills

AGE GROUP(S): 4 & older

This can be an individual project or a group. The bricks can be completed in a day but need several hours to dry. Whatever construction design you choose can take as long as you like, we did a small building over the course of a few weeks.

MATERIALS: Dirt, sand, water & hay or straw; books on adobe making with photos; Ice trays, shoe boxes, plastic and/or cardboard. Depending on the size of the bricks, use ice trays for smaller and shoe boxes for larger one. Determine ahead of time what you will make so you will have enough trays to make the bricks. Another item to use would be the cardboard boxes that have the section pieces in them. These work really well.

ENVIRONMENT: Outside, near a water hose or faucet; patio area, or just in the dirt. This is an amazing project!

DIRECTIONS: Discuss with the children the process of making adobe bricks; decide on what you would like to create and how many bricks will be needed.

Each child places a half of shovel of soil into the large container. Break up the dirt with your hands and throw the rocks in the small bucket.

Break up the soil and crumble the clumps. Do the twist dance on the soil until it is fine.

Continue crushing the dirt to fine powder. Add equal amounts of sand. Mix well with your hands.

Each child then adds one handful of straw. Mix well. This is the binder that binds the brick together.

Add enough water to make a mush-like mixture. Mix well with hands.

Fill the adobe brick mold with the mixture. Pat with your fingers and fists and smooth the top with the wooden trowel. Bake in the sun for several hours until hardened. You have just created adobe bricks and can now build something!

NOTES: This is a messy project, but so much fun. Determine ahead of time what you and the children would like to make, this can be used for group work, or individual. Either way creating a small house or structure will be amazing. If a child likes animals, make a barn; or a doll house, anything can be accomplished. This experiential is wonderful for building more positive family relations.

RESOURCES:
http://www.beniciahistoricalmuseum.org/edu_hands.htm#ADOBE\

House of Adobe (Native Dwellings) by Bonnie Shemie
This House is made of Mud (Esta hecha de lado) by Ken Buchanan.

EXPERIENTIAL: Tree Branch Painting on Floor Cloth

OBJECTIVES:

- Enhance fine motor skills
- Develop Kinesthetic Awareness
- Develop Concept Awareness
- Increase social interaction
- Increase self esteem/self efficacy
- Encourage Language and Communication Skills

AGE GROUP(S): 3 & older

MATERIALS: Paper plates for paint, green, brown yellow, white, blue; you can use several colors, or just 2 or 3. I allow the children to pick whatever colors they want. Floor cloth; comes in a tube and cost about $14. It is a large canvas that is already primed, and can be purchased at Michaels. This is wonderful to use for a painting that will last a lifetime and you can have it framed.
You will have to flatten the floor cloth out first.
Tree branches: pine trees, eucalyptus, mesquite…

ENVIRONMENT: Outside or inside, large work area (outside is preferable, can be messy).

DIRECTIONS: Let the children know that they will be using a variety of tree branches to paint with. Have a table or work area where you can set out the plates and branches on; and where the children can move freely.
Direct the children to just brush the branch over the paint and then onto the floor cloth.

The children will usually ask to use their hands after using the branches; this is just another way for a child to play and experience the paint. I will allow the children to do this, but after they experience the tree branches, and follow directions.

NOTES: You can use butcher paper, white or brown. You just need a large area to work on. You can also use fabric, such as an old sheet. You can hang up the paper, cloth or sheet on a wall for the kids to paint if you do not have a large enough work space. This is a great project, and one that the children will be very proud of.

I have used this experiential and found it to be useful with children who have aggressive behaviors; it provided an outlet for expressing feelings.

EXPERIENTIAL: Mandalas

OBJECTIVES:

- Enhance fine motor skills
- Encourage language and communication
- Increase social skills
- Develop conceptual awareness/spatial ability
- Develop kinesthetic awareness
- Increase self esteem/self efficacy

AGE GROUP(S): 3 & older

MATERIALS: Large sheet of paper; markers, colored pencils, roller paints

ENVIRONMENT: Table or floor

DIRECTIONS: Have the circle or Mandala already drawn on the paper with sections; depending on how many children will be working on it at the same time (no more than 4 for older children, and 2-3 for younger). The more children that are participating, the larger the paper should be. Have your supplies within easy reach, instruct the children to draw or create whatever they want. Let the children know that they can use paint, markers, and pencils. You can have a design already on the Mandala, or you can use a blank slate.

NOTES: You can show pictures of Mandalas to encourage creativity. Sometimes when you give a child a blank space, it can be intimidating; but when you work alongside a child, he/she will get right in there with you and start creating. This is a fun, creative activity for children with Autism; I did it with younger and older children.

I had two 3 year old boys with Autism work on a Mandala together, they showed enthusiasm, shared the materials, engaged in verbal communication, and had a lot of fun. This was also used with a group of older girls, with great success!

(See example on front cover; Mandala Experiential: "Where do you go in the eye of the storm"?)

PAINTING EXPERIENTIALS

Dot Painting
Easel Painting
Creative T- Shirts
Half and Half Paintings

Painting with dots created by a 5 year old boy

Painting by a 4 year old boy with Autism

EXPERIENTIAL   Painting with Dots

(Source: Paint! Art Activities for Kids by Kim Solga, p.16, Dots of Color).

OBJECTIVES:

- Attention to task/following directions
- Use of a different tool and technique
- Increase concept development
- Increase concentration and task completion
- Increase fine motor skills

AGE GROUP(S):   Any age

MATERIALS: Cue Tips – Bright Colored Paint – White paper preferably a card stock with an image of a fish, flower, car; or blank paper if the child wants to create his/her own image. Have plenty of cue tips available for use and a small garbage can for disposal of used cue tips.

ENVIRONMENT: Table Top – Classroom – Home
Work area should be free of clutter and materials laid out for easy access

DIRECTIONS: Have a variety of paint colors poured onto a paper plate; direct child to work only with dots using the cue tips. You can show a sample completed picture to the child as this will encourage and motivate to follow the directive.

NOTES: Encourage the individual to complete the task, do parallel work with the child using a picture of your own. This activity is important for task completion, attention span and following directions.

EXPERIENTIAL: Easel Painting

OBJECTIVES:

- Increase fine motor skills
- Enhance tactile/kinesthetic awareness
- Develop conceptual awareness
- Develop spatial awareness
- Develop language/communication skills

AGE GROUP(S):   3 & older

MATERIALS: Easel, paint, brushes, cup of water, palette, paper towel and paper; sponges

ENVIRONMENT: Inside or Outside

DIRECTIONS: Have supplies laid out for easy access, have a variety of brushes, sizes and textures. Ask the child what colors he/she would like to use, pour onto palette. Talk to the child about painting, mixing colors, etc. and work alongside the child. As the child starts to paint on his/her own, fade yourself out. Allow the child to take as much or as little time possible.

NOTES: Using an easel helps when a child is resistant or reluctant to paint; it is something different, and having a variety of brushes helps with tactile awareness. Talk with the child about the different brushes and demonstrate what each one can do. Talk about blending colors and ask the child "if I mix blue and yellow, what will I get", this is a great opportunity to encourage language skills. Of course use age appropriate questions and your imagination. Whenever I work with a child with autism, or any child, I never tell them what to do, I will give some instruction, demonstrate, and encourage. I allow the child to do as much on his/her own and observe. I acquire most of the information I need to assist a child, by observation.

EXPERIENTIAL: Half & Half Painting
(Source: Paint! Art & Activities for Kids by Kim Solga (pp.38-39)

OBJECTIVES:

- Increase language/communication skills
- Increase fine motor skills
- Increase concept development
- Enhance tactile/kinesthetic awareness
- Encourage creativity

AGE GROUP(S):   5 & older

MATERIALS: Magazine photos (pre-cut), paints, paper, scissors, glue, paint brushes

ENVIRONMENT: Table, work area free of clutter. Have pictures displayed on paper plates or in zip lock bags. Have supplies available so the child can have easy accessibility.

DIRECTIONS: Discuss the project with the child, and work alongside. You and the child can choose a photo to use and glue it wherever you would like on the paper. Then instruct the child to paint, blending the painting with the photo. You can be as creative as you want with this activity.

NOTES: If you are working with older children, they can cut out their own photos.
You can also arrange your supplies in such a way to encourage the child to ask for something. This is part of why observation is so important. These are great learning opportunities for the child to develop requesting skills in language/communication development.

Half & Half Painting

Created by a 10 year old boy with Autism

EXPERIENTIAL: Creative T - Shirts

OBJECTIVES:

- Increase fine motor
- Enhance tactile/kinesthetic awareness
- Develop conceptual awareness
- Develop spatial awareness
- Develop language/communication skills
- Increase self esteem/efficacy

AGE GROUP(S):   3 & older

MATERIALS: 100% cotton t-shirt, fabric paint (non-toxic), a variety of shapes made out of sponges (you can purchase a bag from Michaels), paper plates for paint. Michaels also has a fabric paint in a tube that you can have the child use to squeeze out and make designs with if the child is resistant to putting his/her hands in the paint. You can also use different shape sponges if the child is resistant to help the child get used to working with the paints. Cardboard or brown paper bags to slip into the tee shirt; and some plastic hangers. This can also be done with fabric markers, name writing, signing a peers t-shirt; drawing a picture(s); anything the individual wants to do.

DIRECTIONS: Discuss with child what you will be doing, place cardboard or paper bags into tee shirt, use sponges, or design with squeeze bottles of paint, hand prints, or some of each.

Hang tee shirt up to dry and allow at least 24hrs. Wash in cold water on delicate, mild soap and hang dry before wearing.

NOTES: This is a great activity for a child to gain pride of ownership, he/she will be proud to wear this! If the child is hesitant to put hands in paint, you can demonstrate or do hand over hand if you want hand prints. Often the child will be resistant, but just explain that you can wash your hands when done. You can also create tie dye t-shirts. This activity was done with a 4 year old who was at first hesitant to put his hands in the paint to create the handprint. However, he allowed me to paint his hands which helped him to complete the project. This is an important piece to remember when working with children with autism; not to give up but to find a different way to get the child to engage in the activity without forcing. I touched his hand first to show him how I would paint his hand and this made him laugh. This encouraged him to complete the activity.

Collaboration with child and instructor

SPECIAL OCCASSIONS EXPERIENTIALS

Painting & Collage Christmas Picture
Christmas Cards
Woven Paper Father's Day Cards

Christmas tree Picture

Christmas Cards

EXPERIENTIAL: Painting & Collage Christmas Picture
Christmas Cards

OBJECTIVES:

- Increase fine motor skills
- Increase concept awareness
- Develop language and communication
- Develop spatial abilities
- Enhance tactile/kinesthetic awareness
- Increase knowledge of holiday and giving
- Increase attention span
- Pride of ownership

AGE GROUP: 3 & Older

MATERIALS: Have a variety of card stock, scissors, glue, pencils, markers, glitter or anything else you may want to use, as well as some Christmas books.

ENVIRONMENT: Inside at a table large enough to lay out materials

DIRECTIONS: Talk with the child about what you will be doing. Start with the tree, fold the paper in half and show the child how to make the cuts. Card stock works great because it is difficult for the child to tear when cutting; and the child has to work the small muscles a little harder. Then decorate. When I was doing this project, it literally took us an hour. I asked the boy what he wanted to decorate his tree with, so he started to name animals. Then we just cut them out. He glued them on the tree and we just started to cut out shapes. He said he wanted a heart. He had placed a heart on each animal. It was amazing to watch, an "ah ha" moment.

NOTES: The next day we made the cards. I assisted with some of the cutting of animals but the child did about 85% of the work on his own. Let the child draw or do whatever he/she wants. Remember, directed activities are necessary; but we want to allow the child to do as much as he/she is able and/or willing to do.

EXPERIENTIAL: Woven Paper Father's Day Cards (or any other celebration)

OBJECTIVES:

- Increase fine motor skills
- Increase concept awareness
- Develop language and communication
- Develop spatial abilities
- Enhance tactile/kinesthetic awareness
- Increase knowledge special occasions and giving
- Increase attention span

AGE GROUP(S):   7 & older

MATERIALS: Card Stock, markers, magazines, glue, scissors, colored pencils and a paper cutter if available and only to be used by an adult.

ENVIRONMENT: Table area with lots of room to spread out supplies.

DIRECTIONS: Have strips of paper pre-cut in a variety of colors and two different sizes, 5 x7 or 8 x 10. Instruct the child to place a line of glue down the side of paper, then start placing strips in horizontal order, only glue the left side about ¼ inch from the edge, then start to weave strips of alternating color. Glue the strips where they overlap. Decorate.

NOTES: There are many options for creativity in this project, it is important to have a variety of items available for the child. Encourage the child to use words as well as pictures.

This is an activity I created during an experiential in Expressive Arts; this turned out to be a great activity for many of the children I have worked with. During the creation of the Father's Day card shown below, several children participated, and this activity emerged into one of the most relaxing for all.

Woven Paper Card

Created by a 10 year old boy with autism,
He completed 95% of the weaving on his own.

References

Banks, S., Davis, P., Howard, V.F., & McLaughlin, T.F. (1993) "The effects of directed art activities on the behavior of young children with disabilities: A multi-element baseline analysis." *Art Therapy: Journal of the American Art Therapy Association,* 10(4), 235-240.

Brown, J. (2000). Flat Stanley

Edwards, C., Gandini, L., Forman, G. (1998). the Hundred Languages of Children the Reggio Emilia Approach-Advanced Reflections 2nd Ed. Alex Publishing Corp., Westport, CT.

Flowers, T. (1992) Reaching the Child with Autism through Art. *Practical, "fun" Activities to enhance motor skills and improve tactile and concept awareness* Future Horizons: Arlington, TX.

Jones, E., & Reynolds, G. (1992) The Plays the Thing: Teachers' Roles in Children's Play. Teachers College Press, Columbia University

Knill, P. J., Nienhaus Barba, H., & Fuchs, M. N. (2004) Minstrels of Soul *Intermodal Expressive Therapy* 2nd Ed. E.G.S. Press, Toronto, Ontario M4K IN2 Canada.

Lovaas, O. I., & Smith, T. (1989). A comprehensive behavioral theory of autistic children: Paradigm for research and treatment. *Behavioral Therapy and Experimental Psychiatry, 20,* 17-29.

Miller, K. L. (2005-2008). Love You Doll Kit. Original Presents, LLC

Rasmussen, C. H. (1995). Sensory Integration Retrieved July 14th, 2007, from: http://www.autism.com.

Reber, A. S., & Reber, E. S. (2001) Dictionary of Psychology Penguin Books: London, England.

References Continued

Solga, K. (1991). Paint! Art Activities for Kids. F & W Publications, Inc.: Cincinnati, OH.

Volkmar, F. R., & Pauls, D. (2004) Autism Lancet, *362*, 1133-1141.

Vygotsky, L. S. (1978). Mind in Society: *The development of higher psychological processes.* Cambridge, MA: Harvard University Press.

WEBSITES

http://dictionary.reference.com

http://www.mandalas.com

http://www.oclda.org/sensory.html

http://www.pleasanton.k12.ca.us/valley_view/second/wolfe/stan/makeStanley.hm

http://www.beniciahistoricalmuseum.org/edu_hands.htm#ADOBE

All photographs were taken by this writer, special permission per Release/Waiver forms were obtained for use in this book strictly for educational purposes. Many thanks to all of the sources I have cited within this book; your work has helped in the creation of my work with children with Autism to demonstrate how they too can create art. Very special thanks to Jessica Neel, my daughter-in-law for editing this book; you have been a tremendous help and support.

"When I examine myself and my method of thought,
I come to the conclusion that the gift of fantasy has meant more to
me than my talent for absorbing thought"
Albert Einstein

My Name is a Tree – This Inspired Me

Experiential on Canvas

CPSIA information can be obtained
at www.ICGtesting.com
229500LV00005B

9 781453 641415